CHEERLEADING

Don Wells

WEIGL PUBLISHERS INC.

Published by Weigl Publishers Inc.
350 5th Avenue, Suite 3304, PMB 6G
New York, NY USA 10118-0069
Copyright 2006 Weigl Publishers Inc.
www.weigl.com

Library of Congress Cataloging-in-Publication Data

Wells, Donald.
  For the love of cheerleading / by Don Wells.
     p. cm. -- (For the love of sports)
  Includes index.
  ISBN 1-59036-295-0 (hard cover : alk. paper) -- ISBN 1-59036-299-3 (soft cover : alk. paper)
  1. Cheerleading--United States--Juvenile literature. I. Title. II. Series.
  LB3635.W45 2006
  791.6'4--dc22

                                    2004029001

Printed in The United States of America

1 2 3 4 5 6 7 8 9 09 08 07 06 05

All of the Internet URLs given in the book were valid at the time of publication. However, due to the dynamic nature of the Internet, some addresses may have changed, or sites may have ceased to exist since publication. While the author and publisher regret any inconvenience this may cause readers, no responsibility for any such changes can be accepted by either the author or the publisher.

Project Coordinator

Tina Schwartzenberger

Substantive Editor

Frances Purslow

Design

Warren Clark

Layout

Kathryn Livingstone

Photo Researcher

Kim Winiski

Photograph credits
Cover: Louisiana State University cheerleaders entertain fans during basketball tournament (Doug Pensinger/Getty Images)

Getty Images: pages 1 (Doug Pensinger), 3 (Doug Pensinger), 4 (Alfred Eisenstadt/Pix Inc./Time Life Pictures), 5 (PhotoDisc Blue), 6 (Rubberball Productions), 7T (PhotoDisc Green), 7B (Brand X Pictures), 8 (David Liam Kyle/NBAE), 9 (Scott Nelson), 10L (Rob Cianflone/Allsport), 10R (Scott Cunningham), 11 (Al Bello), 12T (Stone), 12B (PhotoDisc Red), 13L (Ronald Martinez), 13R (Donald Miralle), 14 (PhotoDisc Red), 15T (Brian Bahr), 15B (Joe Patronite/Stringer), 16T (Doug Pensinger/Allsport), 16B (Doug Pensinger/Allsport), 17T (Lawrence Lucier), 17B (Craig Jones), 18L (Carlos Alvarez), 18R (Scott Gries), 19L (Dave Benett), 19TR (Time Life Pictures/DMI), 19BR (Darren McCollester/Newsmakers), 20 (FoodPix), 21T (Brian Bahr/Allsport), 21B (PhotoDisc Red), 22 (Andrew D. Bernstein/NBAE), 23 (Photographer's Choice).

Contents

What is Cheerleading?

For centuries, **spectators** have cheered for people playing sports. Still, cheerleading did not **officially** begin until 1898. Johnny Campbell, a student at the University of Minnesota, led the crowd at a football game in a famous cheer. He yelled, "Rah, Rah, Rah! Sku-u-mar, Hoo-Rah! Hoo-Rah! Varsity! Varsity! Varsity, Minn-e-So-Tah!" This cheer is still used. Those who use it today use the name of their team or school.

Cheerleading is more than leading crowds in cheers. Cheerleaders perform **routines** to entertain spectators. They urge players on sports teams to do well.

Cheerleading was a way for college men to show their leadership skills.

The first American cheerleading **squads** performed at colleges in the eastern part of the United States during the 1800s. Squad members were all men.

During the 1970s, cheerleading became a very popular sport. Squads focused on strength and stunts. They **competed** with other cheerleading squads.

By the 1950s, cheerleading had become common in American high schools. Most cheerleaders at this time were girls.

Today, cheerleading is one of the fastest growing sports for girls and women. Cheerleading squads in 43 countries participate in competitions. Nearly 4 million people participate in cheerleading in the United States.

CHECK IT OUT

Read more about the history of cheerleading at

www.nancyredd.com/cheer leading/history.html

What You Will Need

A cheerleader's uniform should be light so he or she can jump, dance, and move quickly. Cheerleaders do not need much equipment to perform their routines.

Cheerleaders wear uniforms with their team or school **logo**.

Women often wear short skirts with matching bloomers, or briefs, underneath. Bloomers are also called "spankies" and "lollies."

Many cheerleaders use pompoms. The first pompoms were made of crepe paper. Around 1965, Fred Gastoff invented vinyl pompoms. **Metallic** red, gold, and blue are the most common pompom colors.

The megaphone can also be an important part of a cheerleader's equipment. A megaphone is a cone-shaped device held to the mouth to boost and direct the voice. Cheerleaders have used megaphones since 1898 to help crowds hear their cheers.

Pompoms come in a variety of bright colors. Usually, they are the team's colors. Pompoms help the crowd see cheerleaders' hand and arm movements.

Cheerleaders wear comfortable shoes such as running shoes or cross-trainers.

Performing

Cheerleaders perform their routines at sporting events such as football or basketball games. They lead the crowd in cheers from the sidelines of the playing field or gym. During breaks in the game, cheerleaders perform longer routines. Their performances keep the crowd excited about the game.

Cheerleaders perform at **pep rallies** and other school events to promote school spirit. Routines can be performed in school auditoriums, lunchrooms, gyms, or sports stadiums.

Cheerleaders amaze crowds at sporting events with their skills and stunts.

Cheerleading competitions usually take place on a stage. Squads that compete perform **tumbles** and other complicated movements on mats. Mats help prevent injuries.

Some cheerleaders, including this group from the Baltimore Ravens, entertain American soldiers serving overseas.

Cheerleading Basics

There are two types of cheerleaders: spirit squads and competitive teams. Spirit squads cheer for sports teams and perform at sporting events. Competitive teams, also called drill teams, usually perform at competitions. Some competitive teams also perform at sporting events.

Spirit squads use chants and cheers to keep the crowd interested in the game and encourage their team. Spirit squads use tumbling, lifts, tosses, and dance moves set to music to entertain the crowd.

Cheers or chants are often done to specific dance moves.

Cheerleaders display impressive balance and strength in their routines.

C ompetitive teams develop and perform **synchronized** 2- or 3-minute routines. Coaches often **choreograph** and help squads rehearse the routines. Competitive teams also use tumbling, lifts, tosses, and dance moves set to music.

In some routines, strong cheerleaders, called bases, lift smaller cheerleaders, called flyers. Flyers are sometimes thrown high into the air and caught before they hit the ground. Cheerleading squads also build human pyramids. During competitions, competitive teams receive scores for their routines from judges. The winner is the squad with the highest team score.

Cheerleaders often perform dangerous moves and stunts. They do not wear **protective** gear. To help prevent injuries, the National Federation of State High Schools Association created safety rules for all American school-based cheerleading squads. These rules cover all **techniques** cheerleaders use.

Cheerleaders must learn to trust their teammates. All members rely on each other for safety.

CHECK IT OUT

Find cheerleading tips, basic information, photos, and routines at

www.americancheerleader.com

Moves and Stunts

Cheerleaders must have coordination and a good sense of timing. They must be able to perform tumbling and dance moves as well.

Cheerleaders perform **precise** movements. All members of a squad often make the same motions at the same time. Cheerleaders add small changes to basic motions to make the movements more entertaining. Cheerleaders also use **gymnastic** moves with many jumps in their routines.

A cupie is a base standing with a fully extended arm holding a flyer above his or her head. This is also called an awesome.

In the toe-touch jump, the cheerleader's legs are in the splits position, lifted as high as possible.

Cheerleading routines often involve stunts performed by two or more cheerleaders. Specially trained coaches teach stunts. Cheerleaders use **spotters** who can catch them if they fall while attempting a stunt.

One stunt is called the cradle. Several cheerleaders act as bases and throw a flyer who is standing on the bases' hands into the air. The flyer rises into the air and lands back in the bases' arms. Another stunt is the elevator. The bases push a flyer up until their arms are straight above their heads.

Flyers must time their acrobatic moves perfectly so the bases can catch them safely.

Many cheerleading squads include dance moves and music in their routines.

CHECK IT OUT

View photos of outstanding stunts at

www.cheerleadingstunts. net/cheerleadingstunts pictures.asp

Cheerleading Groups

The United States has many cheerleading **organizations**. Most of these groups try to make cheerleading a safe sport.

In 1948, Laurence "Hurkie" Hurkimer founded the first cheerleading organization, the National Cheerleading Association (NCA). He organized the first cheerleader camp at Sam Houston University in Huntsville, Texas. Fifty-two girls attended the camp. Within a few years, 20,000 girls were attending Hurkimer's camps.

The NCA now sponsors championships for all levels of cheerleading squads. The most important event hosted by the NCA is the Chick-fil-A Cheer and Dance Collegiate Championship. More than 140 university cheerleading squads from the United States, Canada, Japan, and Mexico compete in this competition. It is shown on network television.

Many cheerleaders attend camps and workshops to perfect their moves and stunts.

CHECK IT OUT

You can find valuable advice on creating cheer routines at

http://cheerleading.lifetips.com

A cheerleader from the University of Kansas, Randy L. Neil, established the International Cheerleading Foundation (ICF) in 1964. The ICF hosted the first nationally televised cheerleading competition in 1978. The ICF became the World Cheerleading Association (WCA) in 1995. The WCA has members in the United States, England, Germany, Ireland, and Scotland. More than 5,000 cheerleading squads have competed at the WCA Nationals.

Jeff Webb, a cheerleader at the University of Oklahoma, founded the Universal Cheerleaders Association (UCA) in 1974. The UCA started the National High School Cheerleading Championships in 1979.

The National Collegiate Athletic Association, which oversees all college sports, does not consider cheerleading a sport.

More than 220 U.S. colleges offer cheerleading scholarships.

Professional Cheerleaders

The first professional sports team to have cheerleaders was the National Football League's (NFL) Baltimore Colts. The Colts introduced cheerleaders in 1960.

The Washington Redskins cheerleaders are the oldest active cheerleading squad in the NFL. The squad, called the Redskinettes, was formed in 1962. Besides cheering for the Redskins, the cheerleaders have raised millions of dollars for charity. They have toured China to promote U.S.-made products. They have even entertained U.S. military troops serving in foreign countries.

While games are in play, professional cheerleaders entertain from the sidelines.

The Washington Redskins cheerleaders are also known as the "First Ladies of Football."

In 1972, the Dallas Cowboys cheerleaders added Broadway-style jazz dancing to their cheerleading routines. When the Dallas Cowboys cheerleaders appeared on television at Super Bowl X in 1976, the public became more aware of professional cheerleaders. After this event, most NFL teams created cheerleading squads. Each NFL cheerleading team has 30 members.

Basketball cheerleaders are often called dancers. Unlike the NFL, the number of cheerleaders on basketball cheerleading teams varies. Many professional cheerleading squads also offer junior teams.

Tryouts for professional cheerleading teams are very competitive. Hundreds try out for very few positions.

The average career for a professional cheerleader lasts 5 years.

Cheerleading Superstars

Cheerleaders entertain fans and amaze crowds with their tumbling and dance moves. Many famous people have been cheerleaders.

HALLE BERRY

BIRTH DATE:
August 14, 1968
HOMETOWN:
Cleveland, Ohio

Career Facts:

- Halle is an Oscar-winning actress who has starred in films such as *X-Men* and *Catwoman*.
- Halle was a cheerleader at Bedford High School in Cleveland.

SAMUEL L. JACKSON

BIRTH DATE:
December 21, 1948
HOMETOWN:
Washington, D.C.

Career Facts:

- Samuel is a well-known actor who has starred in many films, including *The Incredibles*, *Star Wars Episode I*, and *Star Wars Episode II*.
- Samuel was a cheerleader at his high school in Chattanooga, Tennessee.

PAULA ABDUL

BIRTH DATE:
June 19, 1963
HOMETOWN:
San Fernando,
California

Career Facts:

- Paula is a well-known choreographer, singer, and songwriter.
- Paula was captain of the Van Nuys High School cheerleading squad in Van Nuys, California.
- Paula was a professional cheerleader for the Los Angeles Lakers basketball team.

MERYL STREEP

BIRTH DATE:
June 22, 1949
HOMETOWN:
Summit, New Jersey

Career Facts:

- Meryl is an Oscar-winning actress. She has starred in films such as Lemony Snicket's A Series of Unfortunate Events and The Manchurian Candidate.
- Meryl was a cheerleader at Bernardsville High School in New Jersey.

GEORGE W. BUSH

BIRTH DATE:
July 6, 1946
HOMETOWN:
New Haven,
Connecticut

Career Facts:

- George served as the 43rd president of the United States.
- George was head cheerleader when he attended the all-boys Phillips Academy in Andover, Massachusetts.

CHECK IT OUT

Discover other famous cheerleaders by visiting

http://cheerleading.about.com/od/famouscheerleaders

Staying Healthy

Cheerleading requires jumping, tumbling, and other types of **energetic** movements. A healthy diet is important for cheerleaders.

Eating carbohydrates like bread, pasta, whole grains, vegetables, and fruits provides cheerleaders with energy. Protein from meat and eggs builds muscles. Calcium in dairy products also keeps bones strong.

Drinking plenty of water before, during, and after cheerleading routines is important. Water helps keep people's bodies cool. When cheerleaders sweat, they lose water. Drinking water replaces what is lost through sweat during a routine. Cheerleaders should avoid sugary drinks.

Eating a wide variety of healthy foods, including whole-grain bread, fruits, vegetables, and milk products, is an important part of any diet.

To hold poses and perform stunts, cheerleaders need strong muscles.

Cheerleaders need strong, flexible muscles. Stretching keeps muscles flexible. It is best to stretch after a **warm up**. Running in place or jogging warms muscles and helps prevent injuries.

Cheerleaders should avoid doing routines on hard surfaces. It is easy to twist an ankle while performing cheerleading routines. Wearing heel inserts in shoes can help reduce the risk of foot and ankle injuries. Wearing cross-trainers with good support helps, too.

Cheerleaders must be flexible to perform high kicks and leg lifts.

CHECK IT OUT

Learn more about the importance of flexibility in cheerleading at
http://cheerleading.about.com/od/flexibility/l/bltips_flexible.htm

Cheerleading Brain Teasers

Test your knowledge of this exciting sport by trying to answer these cheerleading brain teasers!

Q When did cheerleading officially start?

A Cheerleading officially started in 1898 at the University of Minnesota.

Q Where do cheerleaders perform routines?

A Cheerleaders perform in school auditoriums, gyms, and on sports playing fields.

Q Name two pieces of equipment used by cheerleaders.

A Cheerleaders often use pompoms and megaphones.

Q What are the two types of cheerleading squads or teams?

A The two types of cheerleading squads are spirit squads and competitive teams.

Q What types of skills do cheerleaders need to join a cheerleading squad?

A Cheerleaders should know how to do precision movements, gymnastics, tumbling, and dance.

Q Which professional cheerleading squad was the first to add Broadway-style jazz dancing to cheerleading routines?

A Cheerleaders for the Dallas Cowboys football team began using jazz dancing in their routines in 1972.

Glossary

choreograph: plan cheerleading or dance routines

competed: tried to win

energetic: requiring a large amount of energy

gymnastic: based on the sport, focuses on strength and balance

logo: a symbol that represents a school or sports team

metallic: shiny, looks like metal

officially: formally

organizations: groups of people who work together

pep rallies: events to encourage school spirit

precise: exact

protective: to cover or shield from injury

routines: series of steps or moves

spectators: people who watch something without taking part

spotters: people who watch someone performing a stunt and offer assistance if required

squads: small groups of people who perform routines together

synchronized: perform the same movements at the same time

techniques: specific ways to perform moves in a sport

tumbles: feats such as somersaults, cartwheels, and handsprings

warm up: gentle exercise to get a person's body ready for stretching and game play

Index